Michelangelo

Cover
Holy Family with the Infant Saint John
(Doni Tondo), *1503–1504.*
Galleria degli Uffizi, Florence.

Texts by Valerio Terraroli

Translation by David Stanton

Photograph Credits
Electa Archives, Milan
Foto Musei Vaticani, Rome
Ricciarini, Milan
Saporetti, Milan
Scala Archives, Florence

This volume was printed by Elemond S.p.a.
at the plant in Martellago (Venice) in 1997

Michelangelo

Electa/Art Books International

Michelangelo

I n his *Life of Michelangelo*, published in 1553, Ascanio Condivi wrote that the artist was born at Caprese, in the Tiber Valley, on 6 March 1475 of Francesca di Neri and Ludovico di Leonardo Buonarroti Simoni, the *podestà* (chief magistrate) of Caprese and Chiusi. A few weeks later, having completed his term of office, Michelangelo's father took the family back to Settignano, near Florence.

Since he belonged to a family of the minor nobility, as a boy Michelangelo was able to attend the grammar school of the humanist Francesco Galatea da Urbino in order to train for an administrative career. But soon, through the good offices of the painter Francesco Granacci, he was given the opportunity to become an apprentice in the workshop of Domenico and Davide Ghirlandaio, one of the busiest in Florence—despite the opposition of his family, who considered this choice to be socially demeaning. It is significant that the indenture drawn up between Michelangelo's father and Domenico Ghirlandaio did not contain the traditional provisions. On the contrary, Ludovico Buonarroti requested that his son should start painting immediately without having to study drawing, which he may have already done with Granacci, and that he should receive a higher remuneration than was customary.

The relationship between the boy and Domenico Ghirlandaio was decidedly strained; indeed, Michelangelo refused to recognize that he owed anything to his master. Nevertheless, it was from the latter that he acquired an interest in Masaccio—whose frescoes he studied, as is shown by a famous series of drawings—that led him to explore Tuscan painting as far back as Giotto, aware that he was engaged in cultural regeneration.

This attitude may be explained by the fact that, at this time, he was drawn into the

Jacopino del Conte, *Portrait of Michelangelo*. Casa Buonarroti, Florence.

cultural circle associated with Lorenzo de' Medici.

After only one year of apprenticeship in Ghirlandaio's workshop, apparently because of heated arguments with his master, Michelangelo left in order to be admitted to the much more exclusive Medici garden, in Via Larga, where a splendid collection of antiques and works of art—especially antique medals and cameos—was kept.

After Lorenzo de' Medici's death in 1492 and the expulsion of the Medici, Michelangelo was fascinated by the fiery sermons of Savonarola, the prior of San Marco in Florence, who preached the concept of the reformation of the Catholic Church and Christianity through a process of moralization that, for the whole of the artist's life, formed the opposite pole to the Neoplatonic inspiration in his work. Michelangelo then went to Bologna as a guest of Giovan Francesco Aldrovandi, where, according to his biographers, he began to write poetry and read Petrarch and Dante, of whom he was considered by his contemporaries to be a good exegete, and he had an opportunity to admire the visionary painting of Ercole de' Roberti.

After returning briefly to Florence in 1496, he moved to Rome, where he was a guest of the enlightened court of Cardinal Riario. Here, after immersing himself in antique statuary, he devoted himself exclusively to sculpture: from the *Drunken Bacchus* (Museo del Bargello, Florence) to the *Pietà* (St. Peter's, Rome), without occupying himself with painting, but certainly not neglecting the daily practice of drawing. It was necessary to await 1502, with the election as gonfalonier of the Florentine Republic of Pier Soderini, spokesman of the leading patrician families of the city, for Florence to become an important centre for Italian artists and intellectuals once again. Leonardo da Vinci returned in 1500, Raphael arrived in 1504, curious to find out about all the innovations, and Michelangelo, now famous, returned in 1501. The reason for the latter's return was cogent and prestigious: the proposal to complete a colossal marble statue that had been started by Agostino di Duccio some forty years earlier for the Opera del Duomo (the board of works of the cathedral) and never finished. Depicting David as the symbol of Florentine freedom, it was to be erected in Piazza della Signoria. The undertaking, completed in 1504, established Michelangelo as a sculptor in the eyes of his contemporaries, who observed the extraordinary technical merits and symbolic values of heroic humanity in his work, which was never overwhelmed by the material, but rather was raised to the level of pure idealization.

The first surviving panel painting by Michelangelo that is certainly autograph is the *Holy Family with the Infant Saint John*, known as the *Doni Tondo* (Galleria degli Uffizi, Florence, Plates 1–3). Commissioned for the wedding of Angelo Doni and Maddalena Strozzi, which took place in 1503 or 1504, this work is still closely linked to Quattrocento modes, particularly with regard to the shaped panel or "tondo," the use of tempera and the subject itself. Nonetheless, the iconography was totally transformed by Michelangelo, who showed here that he had understood and reflected on the ideas expressed by Leonardo da Vinci in the cartoon depicting *The Virgin and Child with Saint Anne and Saint John the Baptist* (the Virgin and Child are sitting Saint Anne's lap), especially as regards the pyramidal construction of the group. The iconographic innovations are considerable, beginning with the Virgin, who is depicted without the traditional blue veil; her bare arms, with their powerful musculature, emerge from a classical tunic. Here, however, the composition is very complex, consisting of joints, links and serpentine rhythms that dominate the space and are not assimilated by it as they are in Leonardo's painting. Michelangelo's palette is non-naturalistic due to his choice of bright, smoothly polished colours (these have emerged during the recent restoration and resemble the results obtained on the Sistine Ceiling). The anatomy is not, therefore, a mimesis of reality, but is rather an idealization of humanity, without any distinction between the sexes and typologies, as would later appear in the *Sibyls* (Plate 20) and *Prophets* (Plates 13, 19) in the Sistine Chapel.

The symbolic interpretation, attempted by numerous scholars, identifies Mary and Joseph with the biblical people that has grown up *sub lege*, the law of Moses; dominating the Virgin and the whole scene from above, the Child represents mankind *sub gratia*, and is offered by Joseph to Mary; lastly, although he belongs to the Hebrew people, the infant Saint John intuits the Incarnation of Christ and forms a link between the two spiritual worlds. The spiritual and religious development of mankind depicted here is already, in embryo, what Michelangelo later represented on the Sistine Ceiling. In fact, the nude youths appearing in this painting are, to a certain extent, forerunners of the slaves for the Mausoleum of Pope Julius II and the *Ignudi* on the cornices surrounding the scenes from Genesis (Plates 14, 15) in the Sistine Chapel. They were, however, based on late-Quattrocento Florentine models, as is demonstrated by the studies and works of Pollaiolo and Verrocchio centring on anatomical research, the functional character of line, tension and the exact disposition and form of the muscles.

David, detail. Galleria dell'Accademia, Florence.

Pietà, detail. Museo dell'Opera del Duomo, Florence.

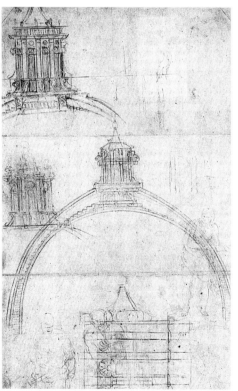

St. Peter's, Vatican, Rome and studies
for the dome.

In the same period, the need to display the moral values of the Florentine Republic in the Council Hall of the Palazzo Vecchio led the republican government to commission a fresco cycle dedicated to the victories of communal Florence; these were symbolically represented by the Battle of Anghiari, entrusted to Leonardo in 1503, and the Battle of Cascina, assigned to Michelangelo in 1504. This work, in which the frescoes of the two leading Tuscan artists of the Cinquecento would have been seen side by side, has not survived, probably because only a portion of the Battle of Anghiari was painted, while nothing more than the cartoon of the Battle of Cascina was executed. Generations of artists acquired their professional skills from these two models, and the interest in, and reverence for, the two works were so unrestrained that, in a short space of time, they had been destroyed. In the surviving copy by Bastiano da Sangallo of the central section of the Battle of Cascina, we find the same parameters used by Michelangelo for his *David*: the hero, facing a dramatic situation, chooses action. It is a stance in sharp contrast with Leonardo's cosmic pessimism, which identifies the bestiality and ferocity of men and animals that is destined to be annihilated by chaos. On the contrary, a heroic concept of humanity emerges here, and, in this sense it is deeply rooted in the culture of the Florentine Renaissance, which, through faith in civic and moral virtues, redeems itself from brute matter, compares itself with the Godhead, and becomes a protagonist of history.

Michelangelo's Mature Years

In 1503 Giuliano della Rovere became Pope Julius II and, as part of his urban renewal programme invited the leading cultural and artistic figures of the day to

Rome. Michelangelo was summoned in 1505 in his capacity as sculptor in order to design and execute a magnificent tomb for the pope, to be placed in the centre of the new St. Peter's, work on which was about to begin.

The project for the tomb of Julius II, which the pope wanted to equal what was known of the classical tombs, involved Michelangelo from 1505 to 1545 in different stages of design and execution. The first project included a burial chamber around which there was a complex architectural structure having a pyramidal form—crowded with figures from the Old and New Testaments, and Vices and Virtues—that was crowned with the figure of Julius II rising from his sarcophagus. The concept of the progressive redemption of the spirit from matter, in accordance with the principles of Neoplatonism, was expressed by the figures placed at the base. Known as "slaves," various versions of these have survived. In this regard, it has recently been suggested that the unfinished panel by Michelangelo representing the *Entombment* (National Gallery, London) may be linked to the first design of the tomb. It was to have been placed in the burial chamber, which would thus have become both a sepulchre and a synthesis of the arts. The painting certainly belongs to the period between the execution of the *Doni Tondo* and the work on the Sistine Chapel in 1508 and 1509, given that the exceptional formal tension of the figures and the foreshortening of the planes in the earliest sections of the Sistine Ceiling were already to be found in the tondo. The painting evidently reflects the impact that the discovery of the marble group of the *Laocoön* in January 1506 had on Michelangelo, especially with regard to the foreshortening of Christ's body and the pyramidal composition. Moreover, both in the faces of the other figures and in the billowing clouds in the background, it is possible to discern heightened emotivity with Leonardesque overtones.

The rebuilding of the chapel of Sixtus IV (Francesco della Rovere) was planned in 1506 as part of the general renewal of the Vatican palaces. Initially it was only intended to execute the figures of the Apostles in the pendentives linking the walls to the vault, which had been adorned with stars by Pier Matteo d'Amelia and was now to be covered with purely architectural decoration. On the other hand, the walls had already been decorated with frescoes by Botticelli, Perugino, Signorelli, Pinturicchio, Ghirlandaio, Rosselli and Piero di Cosimo in 1483–1485. It was Michelangelo himself (as he states in a letter of 1523) who proposed a more complex and monumental decorative scheme that would firmly link the message of the Old Testament to the contents of the New Testament through the mediation of classical culture represented by the *Sibyls* and the *Ignudi*, which were certainly influenced by his contemporary sculptural studies for the tomb of Julius II. Michelangelo's innovation lay in his total abandonment of any illusionistic preoccupation with the architecture and painted figures that had characterized the Italian painting of the Quattrocento. Work began in 1508 and continued fairly rapidly for four years (with a brief gap in 1511), beginning at the entrance wall and proceeding from the *Stories of Noah* to the *Creation of Eve*, with the respective lunettes depicting the ancestors of Christ. In the first stage, the attention to detail reveals the artist's Florentine training, which becomes less evident towards the final panels, where he displays—in the triptych of the *Creation*—a remarkable capacity for synthesis. By contrast, the lunettes—which did not have an iconographic model—permitted the artist to create a repertoire of human figures whose expressions are variously grotesque, tragic and bizarre, and are always splendidly executed. The recent, much disputed restoration of the ceiling has allowed a close study to be made of Michelangelo's vigorous painting technique, consisting of broad, superimposed brushstrokes. In particular, the artist used a palette that, with its quasi-metallic, iridescent colours and astounding accords, accounts for the plastic tonality of the *Doni Tondo* (Plates 1–3), and finally reveals the matrix of the colours and techniques of the early Mannerists.

The iconographic structure of the Sistine Ceiling (Plate 4) has an architectural division, corresponding to the lunettes and spandrels where the ancestors of Christ from Abraham to Joseph are located (Plates 5–12), while in the four corner pendentives are depicted the miraculous episodes associated with the salvation of the Jewish people: *Judith and Holofernes*, *David and Goliath*, the *Brazen Serpent* and the *Punishment of Haman*. In the lower register of the vault, in great marble thrones, foreshortened and delimited by classical sculptures are seated the *Sibyls* and *Prophets* with their powerful limbs (Plates 13, 19, 20). Finally, in the central area, alternating with arches, marble cornices and bronze medallions—on which are represented figures of *Ignudi* deriving from both the studies for the *Battle of Cascina* and firsthand knowledge of antique sculpture, especially the *Laocoön* and the *Belvedere Torso*—there are nine Bible stories arranged in chronological order: the *Separation of Light from Darkness*; the *Creation of the Sun, Moon and Planets*; the *Separation of the Earth from the Waters*; the *Creation of Adam*; the *Creation of Eve*; the *Fall of Adam and Eve* (Plate 14); the *Sacrifice of Noah*; the *Deluge* (Plate 15);

the *Drunkenness of Noah*. From the entrance, the visitor sees these frescoes in the opposite order to the chronological one, but in the sequence in which they were executed. It almost seems as if the artist wished to accompany the viewer on the emotional and symbolic journey of the soul towards God.

The overall theme is, therefore, that of the revelation of God: in the lunettes and spandrels the artist depicts titanic human beings who are still without his light; in the series of *Prophets* and *Sibyls*, on the other hand, the message of salvation, still in an embryonic form, already begins to illuminate their consciences; finally, on the vault, the relationship between man and God becomes direct, almost on equal terms. In any case, it is heroic, with a heroic quality not new to Michelangelo if we think of the nude figures in the *Battle of Cascina* or, even earlier, of the reliefs by Jacopo della Quercia on the main portal of San Petronio in Bologna, which Michelangelo had admired and studied.

The recent restoration has clearly revealed the structural importance of the architecture, which is very closely related to the figures, as had been intended in the project for the tomb of Julius II. It was not, however, real architecture conforming to the traditional canons of the Renaissance: on the contrary, the cornices on which the *Ignudi* rest (Plates 16–17) do not converge on a vanishing point, but diverge, thus suggesting different depths in conflict with each other, as in the monumental thrones of the *Seers* (Plate 13). Everything tends to isolate itself, flouting all the rules of composition. Even the direction of the shadows is not unified, but they are created independently for each figure. What we have here is, therefore, a vision and not a representation, in accordance with the principles of Neoplatonism, which Michelangelo takes to extremes; for him, everything proceeds not according to nature, but in conformity with the inner law of the juxtaposition of contraries that allows us to make a mental link between phenomena that are distant from each other.

From 1534 onwards, after a lengthy period spent in Florence, Michelangelo finally settled in Rome, accepting the commission from Clement VII—then confirmed by his powerful successor Paul III (Alessandro Farnese)—to paint the *Last Judgement* on the end wall of the Sistine Chapel (Plates 22–32). Thus, twenty-three years after finishing the ceiling, the artist returned to the chapel to complete the decorative cycle that had begun with the stories from Genesis. Michelangelo was, furthermore, in tune with the spiritual climate in Rome, which had changed after the Sack of 1527 and the propagation of Lutheran doctrines, and the failure, which affected him profoundly, of the syncretic and positive vision of Neoplatonism. Thus Savonarola's sermons came to mind once more, and the impulse towards the reform of the church regained centrality: the religious crisis was accompanied by a profound existential and aesthetic crisis.

Crucifix, painted wood. Santo Spirito, Florence.

The fresco was completed in 1541 and, once again, gave rise to astonishment and criticism, love and hate. It affected the sensitive nerve-centres of Christian spirituality because it represented the history of mankind terminating with the imperious gesture of Christ the judge, the final arbitrator of good and evil, of grace and eternal salvation. These were the fundamental themes that caused the Christian community to split irretrievably. When painting this work, with its great ideological significance, Michelangelo did not have any help or advice, but he was alone, and, in his solitude, he was only accompanied by the Bible and his ever-loved and

Slave Awakening, Galleria dell'Accademia, Florence.

very familiar Dante. In the same period his long-standing activity as a poet had prompted him to find a kindred spirit in Vittoria Colonna and the Catholic reformist circle that she led, in which faith was considered to be the only road to salvation.

Flouting every iconographic tradition, therefore, Michelangelo created a structure lacking architectural supports and hierarchal and symmetrical order. On the contrary, he created a breathtaking, centrifugal composition in which the prime mover is the awesome figure of Christ the judge bathed in light amidst ample patches of blue sky. The rotary movement begins at bottom left, where the dead rise from their graves to be reunited with the souls and laboriously climb upwards. Like birth, the ascent is painful, uncertain, chaotic and tiring, but the figures are attracted by the divine gesture. Meanwhile, on the right, Christ ordains the violent, headlong fall of the damned, who plummet down into hell and pile up higgledy-piggledy on Charon's bark. The whole composition hangs together thanks to the rhythm of the gestures and bodies, the threatening appearance of the instruments of the Passion wielded by the angels, the terrified expressions of the saints looking towards the centre and the timid gesture of intercession of the Virgin. There is no trace of perspective, colour accords, the classical idealization of the figures, or positive spirituality. On the contrary, the earthy colours of Michelangelo's palette, contrasting with a flat background of sky blue, gives an even more visionary aspect to the scene, which is peopled by the giants of the Sistine ceiling, now old and tired, flabby and abandoned to the intelligible divine plan. The canons of Renaissance painting—and of Mannerism itself—are violated, paving the way for the rhetoric and style of the Baroque. Nevertheless, the reactionary current of the church prevailed in 1542, upsetting the delicate equilibrium and nullifying the modest successes of its internal reformation, leading to a head-on confrontation in which the *Last Judgement* played such a major role. As is well known, the moralizing trend resulted in the periodic painting of draperies on the giant nudes of the *Last Judgement*, which only survived thanks to the enormous prestige as a man of culture that Michelangelo had acquired and consolidated during his lifetime. In the last years of his career, the artist tended to distance himself from painting, as he himself declared in one of his poems, obtaining increasingly non-naturalistic results in sculpture (the *Pietà* in Florence Cathedral, the *Victory* in the Palazzo Vecchio, Florence—a model for the subsequent Mannerist sculpture of Bandinelli and Giambologna—and the *Rondanini Pietà* in the Castello Sforzesco, Milan) and devoting himself principally to architectural projects.

In 1542, while the protagonist of the Catholic Reformation, Cardinal Contarini, was dying, and the Holy Office was being instituted, Michelangelo began his last great pictorial feat: the frescoes in the Cappella Paolina. In fact, while the *Last Judgement* was located in the official centre of Christianity and corresponded to the concept of sacred oratory, the two frescoes painted for Paul III's private chapel represented both the materialization of a sacred lyric and the ultimate crisis of Michelangelo's painting. Adhering to a certain degree to the composition of the *Last Judgement*, in the *Conversion of Saint Paul* (Plates 37–39) the artist expanded the space in the centre of the painting, and then accentuated the centrifugal effect with the foreshortened rearing horse—possibly derived from the

Battle of Cascina—which is linked to the indistinct landscape in the background and the groups of angels above. The action takes place on one side with a daringly foreshortened Christ descending from the sky and the figure of Saul, who has fallen to the ground in a pose clearly echoing that of Heliodorus in Raphael's fresco in the Stanza di Eliodoro. The onlookers, the angels, the landscape and the light move back in order to leave Christ and Saul (who then became the Apostle Paul) alone in a silent and violent colloquy reflected in the grey, earth-coloured palette that leaves no opportunity for purely descriptive elements. Between 1546 and 1550 Michelangelo completed the *Crucifixion of Saint Peter* (Plates 34–36) in which the absence of Christ is noticeable, while, on the contrary, he is dramatically present in the *Conversion*. The high horizon forms the upper limit to the crowded scene where the apostle is alone in the presence of death, without being certain the hereafter awaits him. Silence dominates the whole composition, the pivot of which is the kneeling figure of the digger, borrowed from Masaccio; this echoes and counterbalances the curve of Peter's body, who almost seems to be rebelling against his fate. The highly dramatic sense of this painting was only fully comprehended some fifty years later, when Caravaggio painted the *Crucifixion of Saint Peter* for Santa Maria del Popolo, Rome, in which the individual tragedy becomes the tragedy of the human predicament.

In the final years of his life Michelangelo devoted himself entirely to architecture: the completion of the new St. Peter's, with a huge dome that, based on Brunelleschi's projects, had a centrifugal design, materializing in marble the movement of the *Last Judgement*; and Santa Maria degli Angeli, converted from the huge hall of the Baths of Diocletian, in which his role was a non-interventionist one, the ultimate alternative to representing and transforming visual reality.

His increasing concern with religious issues, old age and the crisis of aesthetic values brought Michelangelo into contact with the Catholic reformist circle of Vittoria Colonna, for whom, around 1545, he drew, and possibly painted, a *Crucifixion* (Plate 33). A number of outstanding studies for the figures of the *Mater Dolorosa* and *Saint John* have survived; direct descendants of the fearsome figures of the *Last Judgement*, they are isolated, without the light of grace, as in the Cappella Paolina.

Until the very last days of his life Michelangelo was working on the *Rondanini Pietà*; he died at his home in Rome near the Forum of Trajan on 18 February 1564. His influence was felt throughout the century, giving rise to artistic experimentation fraught with consequences for the future, while his life, always torn between the two opposite poles of humanism and a strong moralizing predisposition, concluded with the final defeat of the idea that art is mimesis, in accordance with Aristotelian theories, and an awareness of the fundamental impossibility of the reconciliation between the history of humanity, splendid as it was even in sin, and the inscrutability of the divine plan.

Where to See Michelangelo's Works

Michelangelo's career was divided between Florence and Rome: as might be expected, the vast majority of his works—whether of sculpture, painting or architecture—may be seen in these two cities. There are very few exceptions, and only a very limited number of his sculptures are to be found outside Italy, which is quite unusual for a Renaissance artist.

Works in Italy

In *Florence* there could be many starting points for a tour of places associated with Michelangelo, but the most fascinating is probably the Casa Buonarroti, near the Church of Santa Croce.

Purchased and rebuilt by one of the artist's nephews, for over three centuries it has been a museum and monument dedicated to the many-sided career of Michelangelo. Amidst relics, commemorative paintings and portraits of the artist, a number of outstanding original works are worthy of note. These include a series of drawings of figures and architectural studies, mainly relating to the Church of San Lorenzo. In addition, there is an interesting group of early sculptures: the *Madonna of the Steps* and the *Battle of Lapiths and Centaurs*, both in marble, a wooden *Crucifix*, a small *David* in bronze, and maquettes for a *River God* and *Hercules* and *Cacus*.

Although there are no works by Michelangelo in Santa Croce, it is worth a visit because it houses the artist's tomb, a magnificent work by Giorgio Vasari.

Proceeding towards the city centre, the visitor reaches the Galleria degli Uffizi, where there is the only panel painting that may be attributed with certainty to the artist, the *Holy Family with the Infant Saint John*, known as the *Doni Tondo*. Also worthy of attention is the series of antique sculptures displayed in the corridors. Some of these were certainly studied by Michelangelo during his youth when he frequented the Medici garden, although some may have been restored or added to (the *Flaying of Marsyas*, for instance). In the Gabinetto dei Disegni, moreover, there are a number of Michelangelo's most outstanding drawings.

The most important room in the Palazzo Vecchio, the Sala dei Cinquecento, houses the lithe and vigorous *Victory*, a sculpture that is particularly significant for its influence on the subsequent development of Mannerism. Among the works retrieved by Rodolfo Siviero, also in the Palazzo Vecchio, there is a *Bust of Christ*; this is believed to be a part of the *Rondanini Pietà* that was then removed.

Of fundamental importance is the next port of call, the Museo Nazionale del Bargello, with its splendid collection of marble statues. The most famous is the *Bacchus*, a masterpiece of Michelangelo's youth, and the first large statue made by the artist. The *Apollo*, believed by some to be David with a sling, is both beautiful and mysterious. The bust of *Brutus* and a relief tondo (the *Pitti Tondo*) complete this important series of works.

The visitor should now proceed to the cathedral, where there is the dramatic group of the *Pietà*, with Michelangelo's famous *Self-portrait as Nicodemus*. A few years ago this sculpture was moved to the Museo dell'Opera del Duomo, behind the apse of the cathedral.

The most remarkable collection of Michelangelo's sculptures is to be found at the Galleria dell'Accademia, where a domed hall has been specially built to house the colossal *David* in marble. Another six works by the artist are on display in the corridor: the unfinished *Saint Matthew*, the only one that was actually started of a series of statues of apostles for the facade of the cathedral; the late *Palestrina Pietà*; and the four *Slaves*, also unfinished. Intended for the tomb of Julius II, the latter are powerful images of the struggle between the figurative concept and the material that surrounds it.

The other area of fundamental importance for Michelangelo's art in Florence is San Lorenzo, the Medici parish church. The New Sacristy, on the right side of the transept, was designed by Michelangelo as the Medici Chapel. A brilliant example of the tension between the elements of architecture, this houses the two symmetrical tombs of Giuliano and Lorenzo de' Medici. In addition to the statues of these two personages, Michelangelo also executed the paired allegories of *Dawn* and *Dusk* and *Night* and *Day*, remarkable for their energy and drama. An outstanding example of the spiral figure is the *Madonna and Child*.

Also forming part of the San Lorenzo complex is the Laurentian Library, an architectural masterpiece: Michelangelo designed the staircase in the entrance hall and the reading room, including even the wooden desks. To complete the tour, the visitor should climb up to San Minia-

to al Monte to observe what has remained of the fortifications designed by the artist when Florence was threatened with a siege. This also allows a visit to Piazzale Michelangelo; the best-known vantage-point in Florence, this is adorned with a nineteenth-century monument attempting to summarize Michelangelo's works, which is as famous as it is kitsch.

The first contact with Michelangelo in *Rome* could well be the Capitoline Hill (Piazza del Campidoglio), a superb example of the combination of urban space, architectural volumes and antique sculptures, which is reached by a spectacular ramp. The beautiful paving irradiates from the statue of *Marcus Aurelius*, imparting regularity to the trapezoidal piazza, at either side of which the palaces of the Museo Capitolino and the Museo dei Conservatori are placed symmetrically. At the end, the Palazzo Senatorio was completed by Giacomo della Porta without conforming entirely to Michelangelo's project (the artist was responsible for the great staircase at the entrance).

Proceeding in the direction of the Colosseum, beyond the Forum, the visitor comes to San Pietro in Vincoli, the ancient church in which stands the *Tomb of Julius II*, a reduced version of the earlier, magnificent projects. Nonetheless, the powerful statue of *Moses*—into whose lap Michelangelo threw his hammer, shouting: "Talk! Why don't you talk?"—suffices to convey the excitement of one of the most remarkable undertakings of the High Renaissance. In the area of the Termini railway station is located the Church of Santa Maria degli

Angeli, which Michelangelo converted from the tepidarium of the Baths of Diocletian in 1566. The attribution to the artist of the adjacent Renaissance convent, now housing the Museo Nazionale Romano, does not, however, appear to be credible.

Not far away is the Porta Pia, built by Michelangelo between 1561 and 1564. This city gate, forming a spectacular conclusion to Via Nomentana, is both a compendium of the vocabulary of Renaissance architecture and its negation. Proceeding from the Capitoline Hill in the direction of the River Tiber, near the Pantheon the visitor will note the Church of Santa Maria sopra Minerva, in which the artist's large *Risen Christ* is situated (1521).

Michelangelo also contributed to the design of the Palazzo Farnese: he was responsible for the central window, the splendid cornice on the facade and the large courtyard. From here it is not far to the Vatican, where the visit should, of course, begin with the Basilica of St. Peter's, the most audacious edifice of the Renaissance. Following in Bramante's footsteps, Michelangelo opted for a central plan, but with specifications and dimensions hitherto unheard of. The whole construction was dominated by a huge dome, the symbol of Christianity. Unfortunately, he did not live to see the completion of his project. In the first chapel on the right there is the exquisite *Pietà*, an early work by the artist and the only one bearing his signature.

The recent restoration has confirmed the fundamental role of the frescoes in the Sistine Chapel in the history of European art. It is important to distinguish between the two stages in which Michelangelo executed the work: the ceiling, commissioned by Pope Julius II, was painted between 1508 and 1512; the *Last Judgement*, on the other hand, was completed under Pope Paul III in 1541. The frescoes are a very personal interpretation of the biblical narratives and one of the great masterpieces of pictorial art. The two frescoes in the Cappella Paolina, the *Conversion of Saint Paul* and the *Crucifixion of Saint Peter*, are, however, less well known.

Other Locations in Italy
A few works by Michelangelo are to be found in other Italian cities. A number of sculptures bear witness to journeys the artist made, especially in his youth, and form part of architectural complexes and sculptural groups. This is the case of the three statuettes in the Church of San Domenico in *Bologna*. *Saint Petronius* and *Saint Procolus* are placed on the edge of the *Shrine of Saint Dominic*, while an *Angel Bearing a Candlestick* is in front of the monument.
In *Siena*, the figures of *Saint Peter* and *Saint Paul* adorn the Piccolomini altar in the cathedral.
In the Castello Sforzesco in *Milan* is the artist's last work, the dramatic *Rondanini Pietà*, which was never completed.
It should be noted that, while numerous drawings by Michelangelo are to be found in the main international collections of Renaissance drawings (especially in London, Boston, Munich and Vienna), very few sculptures have left Italy. The attribution to the artist of a number of panel paintings is still, however, open to debate.

Works Outside Italy
France
In *Paris*, the *Dying Slave* and the *Rebellious Slave*, the only allegorical figures of the original project for the tomb of Julius II to be completed, are in the Louvre.

Great Britain
In *London*, a relief of the *Madonna and Child with the Infant Saint John* (the *Taddei Tondo*) is in the Royal Academy.
In the National Gallery there are two unfinished paintings—the *Entombment and the Madonna and Child with the Infant Saint John and Angels* (known as the *Manchester Madonna*)—that have been attributed to Michelangelo. Moreover, the British Museum possesses one of the most important collections of drawings by the artist.

Belgium
A severe sculpture representing the *Madonna and Child* is on an altar in the Church of Notre-Dame in *Bruges* (also called the *Bruges Madonna*).

Russia
Little known, but of great interest, is a sculpture of a *Squatting Boy* in the Hermitage Museum, *St. Petersburg*.

1

1–3. Holy Family with the Infant Saint John (Doni Tondo), *1503–1504, tempera on circular panel, diameter 120 cm. Galleria degli Uffizi, Florence. The work was executed by Michelangelo for the wedding of Agnolo Doni and Maddalena Strozzi, using a form that was very popular in Florence in the late Quattrocento. The serpentine movement of the figures, the idealized,* classicizing representation *of the Virgin and the smoothly polished, non- naturalistic colours all indicate an artist who was not bound by the traditional schemata and a great experimenter. The figures in the background are considered to be the prototypes of the* Ignudi *in the Sistine Chapel and the* Slaves *for the Tomb of Julius II (Giuliano della Rovere), which, although they belong to the Tuscan humanistic tradition,* are intended here to represent *pre-biblical and pre-Christian humanity in monumental form. The figure of Mary in the* Doni Tondo *corresponds to the human ideal that Michelangelo perfected on the ceiling of the Sistine Chapel, where there is no longer any distinction between male and female, while the monumentality of the figures distances them from realistic representation, transforming them into a pure ideal.*

4–20. Scenes from Genesis, Ancestors of Christ, Prophets and Sibyls, *fresco. Sistine Chapel (ceiling and lunettes), Vatican, Rome. Michelangelo devoted himself to what is universally considered to be his pictorial masterpiece from 1508 to 1512, painting a summary of the history of mankind proceeding from the Mosaic law and the Incarnation of Christ on the shallow barrel-vault of the Sistine Chapel. The plastic bodies of the* Seers *who move, converse animatedly and twist their bodies to observe the epiphany of the Lord are squeezed into the imposing architectural framework that is totally independent of the Renaissance rules of perspective. The iconographic structure of the Sistine Ceiling has an architectural division, corresponding to the lunettes and spandrels where the ancestors of Christ from Abraham to Joseph are located, while in the four corner pendentives are depicted the miraculous episodes associated with the salvation of the Jewish people:* Judith and Holofernes, David and Goliath, *the* Brazen Serpent *and the* Punishment of Haman. *In the lower register of the vault, in great marble thrones, foreshortened and delimited by classical sculptures are seated the* Sibyls *and* Prophets *with their powerful limbs. Finally, in the central area, alternating with arches, marble cornices and bronze medallions—in which are represented figures of* Ignudi *deriving from both the studies for the* Battle of Cascina *and firsthand knowledge of antique sculpture, especially the* Laocoön *and the* Belvedere Torso—*there are nine bible stories arranged in chronological order: the*

EZECHIAS

MANASSES

AMON

5

Separation of Light from Darkness; *the* Creation of the Sun, Moon and Planets; *the* Separation of the Earth from the Waters; *the* Creation of Adam; *the* Creation of Eve; *the* Fall of Adam and Eve; *the* Sacrifice of Noah; *the* Deluge; *the* Drunkenness of Noah. *From the entrance, the visitor sees these frescoes in the opposite order to the chronological one, but in the sequence in which they were executed. It almost seems as if the artist wished to accompany the viewer on the emotional and symbolic journey of the soul towards God. The overall theme is, therefore, that of the*

revelation of God: in the lunettes and spandrels the artist depicts titanic human beings who are still without his light; in the series of Prophets *and* Sibyls, *on the other hand, the message of salvation, still in an embryonic form, already begins to illuminate their consciences; finally, on the vault, the relationship between man and God becomes direct, almost on equal terms. In any case, it is heroic, with a heroic quality not new to Michelangelo.*

5, 6. Lunette of Hezekiah, Manasseh and Haman.
In the fresco cycle in the Sistine Chapel the iconography of the

Ancestors of Christ, *for which Michelangelo did not have any models, is particularly original. The composition with groups of three colossal figures solved the problem of the architectural space of the lunettes — interrupted by the crowns of the window arches and linked to the vault by spandrels — and, with their rhythmic repetition, assumed the symbolic significance of the Trinity. In the detail on the right are clearly visible the remarkable colour innovations — already partially present in the* Doni Tondo — *based on striking contrasts of tones and abrupt, non-naturalistic planes of light.*

7

8

7–9. *Above:* Lunette of Jesse, David and Solomon. *Below:* Lunette of Josiah, Jechoniah and Shealtiel. *The long series of the* Ancestors of Christ *allowed Michelangelo to create a vast range of human types and emotional attitudes from the sublime to the grotesque. In a way, it seems as if he wanted to continue Leonardo's experimentation, but giving it a lucidly non-naturalistic and absolute interpretation.*

12

12. *A detail of one of the lunettes with the* Ancestors of Christ *revealing that Michelangelo was basically not interested in representing the figures realistically. They are, on the contrary, types placed at intervals in space, each of them having different poses and gestures in order to convey the variety of human nature, despite the overall unity.*

13. The Prophet Daniel. *As an architectural link (the monumental thrones) and a symbolic one (the* Prophets *and the* Sibyls*) between mankind before the revelation and the vision of God, Michelangelo placed the great witnesses of the past, biblical and classical, the statuesque figures of which appear to project from the painted architecture.*

DANIEL

14

14, 15. The Fall of Adam
and Eve *(detail) and the*
Deluge *(detail). In the centre
of the ceiling the story of the*
Creation *is represented;
Michelangelo intended to
transform this into both a visual
and spiritual journey. In fact,
the scenes depicting the*
Drunkenness of Noah *and
the* Deluge—*featuring, in other*

*words, weak, unclothed
humanity faced with its own
frailty—are the first that visitors
encounter when entering the
Sistine Chapel. Proceeding
towards the altar, they see the
scenes from* Genesis *in the
opposite order to the
chronological one before
reaching the outstanding central
scene of the* Creation of

Adam, *the definitive
representation of the creation
of man by God in his own image.
Finally, before the altar, there
is the primordial* Separation
of Light from Darkness.
*The cathartic journey concluded,
therefore, with the supreme
vision of Dante: "The love that
moves the sun and the other
stars."*

15

16

16. Study for a Male Nude, *red chalk on paper. One of numerous anatomical studies associated with the* Battle of Cascina, *this drawing is an elaboration of a classical example forming a model for the one of the* Ignudi *seated on the cornice of the ceiling. These idealized nudes can be traced back to the figures in the background of the* Doni Tondo. *They represent, in fact, the Neoplatonic reconciliation of antiquity with the Christian revelation.*

17

17. Ignudo.

19

18. Ignudo *(detail of head).*   *19.* Prophet Joel.

21

20. Delphic Sibyl
(detail of head).
*Under a thick layer of dust,
soot and glue, the recent
restoration has revealed a
brilliant range of colours that
are intentionally clashing and
juxtapositions of bright tones
that eliminate the distance
between the viewer and the
ceiling, constructing a space that*
is not illusorily naturalistic, but
is, on the contrary, a visionary
universe that became a model
for a whole generation of
Mannerists.

21. Head of Cleopatra,
1533–1534, black chalk.
*Casa Buonarroti, Florence.
This drawing was executed
shortly before Michelangelo*
finally left Florence to
settle in Rome, when he was
still searching for ideal
beauty as conceived by
Neoplatonism.
*Nevertheless, in the fantastic
and bizarre style of this head
of Cleopatra there is clearly
an echo of Piero di Cosimo's
so-called portrait of Simonetta
Vespucci.*

23

23. *Drawing for the* Last
Judgement, *black chalk,
34.5 × 29.1 cm.
Musée Bonnat, Bayonne.*

22. *Drawing for the* Last
Judgement, *black chalk,
41.8 × 28.8 cm.
Casa Buonarroti, Florence.
The enormous fresco on the end
wall of the Sistine Chapel
representing the* Last
Judgement *was commissioned
from Michelangelo by Clement
VII in March 1534; this
commission was confirmed by his
successor, Paul III. In order to
paint the fresco Michelangelo*

*had to destroy the frescoes by
Perugino and those in two
lunettes depicting the* Ancestors
of Christ *that he had himself
executed in 1512. In the
drawing, the originality of the
composition—in which, without
architectural supports, clusters
of figures rotate around
Christ—is immediately evident.*

*This is a detail of the upper
portion of the fresco in which
is visible the anatomical study
for Christ clearly derived from
the* Belvedere Torso, *one
of the classical statues with
which Michelangelo was
familiar, while, at the sides,
the composition is still
symmetrical with the two
figures of saints.*

24

24. *Drawing for the* Last
Judgement, *black chalk,*
38.5 × 25.3 cm.
British Museum, London.
This is a sketch for the group of
demons in the lower right corner
of the fresco. Despite the
spontaneity of the line, the power
of these figures is evident; flabby

and without individual
significance, they have sunk
without hope in the dense
materiality of things.

25–32. Last Judgement,
1534–41, fresco,
13.7 × 12.2 m. Sistine Chapel
(altar wall), Vatican, Rome.

This work revolutionized the
traditional scheme divided into
superposed, quite distinct
registers, with Christ enthroned
in the centre. Michelangelo, on
the contrary, created a unified,
tragic space where tangles of
bodies and isolated titanic
figures pile up, fall and

25

laboriously climb up again in an eternal overwhelming rotary movement of ascent and descent, the pivot of which is the colossal figure of Christ the judge, the prime mover of the universe. Besides the forms of the monumental figures—which are, however, heavier and more

flaccid—the earthy colours and ochres attenuate the magnificence of the ceiling painted thirty years previously, heightening the apocalyptic effect of the day of wrath. *The innovations in colour and composition, and the bold foreshortening of the bodies,*

are even more evident in the artist's last pictorial works: the Conversion of Saint Paul *and the* Crucifixion of Saint Peter *for the Cappella Paolina, built for Paul III by Antonio da Sangallo the Younger from 1537 onwards.*

33

33. Crucifixion with the Virgin and Saint John, *black chalk. Ashmolean Museum, Oxford.*
In advanced age, when he became closely associated with the Catholic reformist circle of Vittoria Colonna, Michelangelo executed a Crucifixion *for his friend (perhaps around 1545),* *of which a number of partial studies—and this one of the whole composition—remain. These highlight the artist's progressive abandonment of idealized figures that began with the titans of the* Last Judgement *and concluded with the onlookers in the Pauline frescoes.*

34

34–36. Crucifixion of Saint Peter, 1542–1550, fresco, 6.25 × 6.62 m. Cappella Paolina, Vatican, Rome.
In the frescoes in the Cappella Paolina, nature is not present: rather there is a series of horizons in an airless space flooded with harsh light. And the story is not recounted in an orderly manner, but only with the gathering and dispersion of the groups in an unnatural space, given that there is no gap between the figures on earth and those suspended above. They are nearly all foreshortened, which does not give them greater depth, but appears to remove them from space and squeeze them into their contracted outlines. Note, in particular, the extreme foreshortening, almost a flight towards the horizon, of the horse in the Conversion (but it is balanced by the foreshortened figure of Christ above); and, in the Crucifixion, the kneeling figure of the man digging a hole in which Saint Peter's cross will be placed. Here, in fact, foreshortening is the equivalent of the unfinished sculptural work: the figures neither become part of space nor are they isolated as separate entities, but mingle and fade in this air untouched by time. Rather than depicted they are evoked, reduced to an outline with just a trace of colour. And the colours are lifeless, harsh and clashing; they produce a concert full of intentional dissonance, and their rhythm is extremely irregular, progressing by fits and starts, as in the movement of the figures along the diverging diagonals.

37

37–39. Conversion of Saint Paul, *fresco, 6.25 × 6.61 m. Cappella Paolina, Vatican, Rome.*
The vision of Saul (who was to become the Apostle Paul) on the road to Damascus is Michelangelo's last painting (although it was considerably repainted subsequently); in it, *the rearing horse and the fall of Saul form a counterpoint to the flight of Christ towards the earth surrounded by a choir of astounded and terrified angels. Grace is sudden, unrepeatable and independent of anyone's will; reason finally submits to the inevitability of the divine revelation.*

Anthology of Comments

What good is it sculpting so many statues, / if my art has caused my fate to be that of he, / who crossed the seas and then drowned in his own snot? / Such highly esteemed art, which in the past / brought me great fame, has meant this for me: / that I am poor, old and enslaved to others; / thus I am undone, if I don't die soon.

No block of marble but it does not hide / the concept living in the artist's mind / pursuing it inside that form, he'll guide / his hand to shape what reason has defined. / The ill I flee, the good I hope to find / in you, exalted lady of true pride, / are also circumscribed; and yet I'm lied / to by my art which to my will is blind. / Love's not to blame, nor your severity / disdainful beauty, nor what fortune shows, / or destiny: I fixed my own ill course. / Though death and mercy side by side I see / lodged in your heart, my passion only knows / how to carve death: this is my skill's poor force.
(Girardi, 151. 1538–41/4, in George Bull and Peter Porter, *Michelangelo: Life, Letters and Poetry,* The World's Classics, Oxford University Press, Oxford, 1987.

If with the stylus or colours you have allowed art to match nature, you have removed part of its value, because you represent its beauty in a even fairer way since, with your learned hand, you have devoted yourself to a more noble task, writing, and—what you still lacked— you have obtained part of nature's merit by giving lives to others. Because, if ever any age competed with nature to make beautiful works, it had to resign itself to losing, since each epoch has its appointed end. You, by rekindling memories of others' lives, now faded away, allow these memories, and you with them, to live eternally, in spite of nature herself.
(Michelangelo Buonarroti, *Rime,* ed. by E. N. Girardi, Bari 1960)

Michelangelo wanted to retouch some details *a secco*, as those old masters had done on the scenes below, painting certain fields, draperies, and skies in ultramarine blue and golden decorations in some places to give the painting greater richness of detail and a finer appearance; when the pope understood that this decoration was still missing, having heard the work so highly praised by everyone who had seen it, he wanted this to be provided, but because it would have taken too long for Michelangelo to rebuild the scaffolding, the painting remained as it was. Since the pope saw Michelangelo often, he used to say to him: "Let the chapel be embellished with colours and gold, for it looks too plain." And Michelangelo replied in a familiar tone: "Holy Father, in those days men did not wear gold, and those who are painted there never were rich, for they were holy men who despised wealth."
Michelangelo was paid on account for this work in several instalments, a total of three thousand scudi, of which he had to spend twenty-five on colours. These frescos were done with the greatest discomfort, for he had to stand there working with his head tilted backwards, and it damaged his eyesight so much that he could no longer read

or look at drawings if his head was not tilted backwards; his condition lasted for several months afterwards, and I can testify to this fact, for after working on the vaults of five rooms in the great chambers of the palace of Duke Cosimo, if I had not built a chair upon which to rest my head and to stretch out while I was working, I would never have completed the work, for it ruined my sight and weakened my head to such an extent that I can still feel it, and I am amazed that Michelangelo tolerated such discomfort. But every day kindled even more his desire to work, and with the progress and improvement he made, he neither felt fatigue nor worried about all the discomfort.

(Giorgio Vasari, *The Lives of the Artists*, translated by Julia Conaway Bondanella and Peter Bondanella, The World's Classics, Oxford University Press, Oxford and New York 1991)

In painting other factors should be taken into consideration. In Ghirlandaio's school, Michelangelo only learnt the technique of painting: there is no precedent for his conception of art. The idea of conforming to the expression of devotion, the traditional religious type or the feelings of some other artist was quite foreign to him, and he did not feel that he was bound by this. For him the great wealth of sacred themes in Medieval art did not exist. His man was a new creation with enormous physical strength, who was, in some respects, already demoniac, and with figures of this kind he constituted a new world, earthly and Olympian at the same time. The expressions

and movements of these figures reveal they belong to a generation that is different from all those preceding it. What was characterization in the painting of the Quattrocento has no pretext here because his figures show themselves to be a single unit of their line, or of their people, and individual appearance, if it is required, appears as idealized, superhuman power. Even the beauty of the body and the human face does not appear except in the guise of this power; what mattered to Michelangelo was expression taken to the highest level of vitality, rather than beauty and grace.

(Jacob Burckhardt, *Der Cicerone*, 1855, Florence 1963)

These commonplace beauties, these damaged products, born of a despicable century, these feet suitable for ankle-boots, these fingers ready to play castanets, will never be able to satisfy a heart like mine.

I leave to Gavarni, a poet of chlorosis, his murmuring flock of hospital beauties: among these pale roses, I cannot find a flower that resembles my ideal red.

What is needed for this heart as deep as an abyss is you, Lady Macbeth, the moving spirit of crime, an Aeschylean dream revealing itself in hyperborean climes; O it is you, great Night, born of Michelangelo, who calmly twists, in a strange pose, your forms made for the mouths of Titans.

(Charles Baudelaire, *Les Fleurs du mal,* 1861, Milan 1975)

We are now able to understand why every art whose chief preoccupation is

the human figure must have the nude for its chief interest; why, also, the nude is the most absorbing problem of classic art at all times. Not only is it the best vehicle for all that in art which is directly life-confirming and life-enhancing, but it is itself the most significant object in the human world.

The first person since the great days of Greek sculpture to comprehend fully the identity of the nude with great figure art was Michelangelo. Before him it had been studied for scientific purposes—as an aid in rendering the draped figure. He saw that it was an end in itself, and the final purpose of his art. For him the nude and art were synonymous. Here lies the secret of his successes and his failures.

First, his successes. Nowhere outside of the best Greek art shall we find, as in Michelangelo's works, forms whose tactile values so increase our sense of capacity, whose movements are so directly communicated and inspiring. Other artists have had quite as much feeling for tactile values alone—Masaccio, for instance; others still have had at least as much sense of movement and power of rendering it—Leonardo, for example; but no other artist of modern times, having at all his control over the materially significant, has employed it as Michelangelo did, on the one subject where its full value can be manifested—the nude. Hence of all the achievements of modern art, his are the most invigorating. Surely not often is our imagination of touch roused as by his Adam in the Creation, by his Eve in the Temptation, or by his many nudes in the same ceiling of the Sistine Chapel—there for no other purpose, be it noted, than their direct tonic effect! Nor is it less rare to quaff such draughts of unadulterated energy as we receive from the God Creating Adam, the Boy Angel standing by Isaiah, or—to choose one or two instances from his drawings (in their own kind the greatest in existence)—the Gods Shooting at a Mark or the Hercules and the Lion. And to this feeling for the materially significant and all this power of conveying it, to all this more narrowly artistic capacity, Michelangelo joined an ideal of beauty and force, a vision of a glorious but possible humanity, which, again, has never had its like in modern times. Manliness, robustness, effectiveness, the fulfilment of our dream of a great soul inhabiting a beautiful body, we shall encounter nowhere else so frequently as among the figures in the Sistine Chapel.

Michelangelo completed what Masaccio had begun, the creation of the type of man best fitted to subdue and control the earth, and, who knows! perhaps more than the earth.
(Bernard Berenson, *Italian Painters of the Renaissance*, Phaidon, London 1952, pp. 74–75)

A nd he worked with the claw chisel as if he were using pen and ink on paper. In his drawings, too, he revealed the throbbing life of the human body, the life in the tendons and the skin, going round the body with the close parallel lines of the hatching, or with cross-hatching. And he used the same method with the brush in painting, as the study of the details of the vault of the Sis-

tine Chapel would demonstrate. This principal of interpreting the forms by means of modelling with the constant addition of clarifying lines—a method that appeals to a rational mind—rather than by the pictorial but irrational method of working with light and shade (excluding clearly definable lines) is eminently Tuscan. And Michelangelo was wholly possessed by an investigatory mentality, dedicated to the cogent logic that we associate with the Florentine spirit from the time of Dante. What I am trying to do here may constitute an attempt, possibly a hopeless one, to find the specifically Tuscan roots of Michelangelo's sculptural technique.
(Rudolf Wittkower, *La scultura*, Turin 1985; original title: *Sculpture: Processes and Principles*, London 1977)

T he artist, who emulates nature, must not, therefore, consider the form that is most scorned by nature to be the most beautiful in man. On the contrary, since, of the very beautiful works of nature, the finest and the most pleasing is variety, he must seek to be varied in his work; and if this were not so, he would not please completely. Now observe whether this very necessary aspect is present in Michelangelo's works: all the figures that he paints are large and fearsome. You will point out that the variety lies in their gestures, which are all different from each other. I shall reply that in this very variety there is similarity in the foreshortening, poses and muscles; because Michelangelo thought he had triumphed with great honour over Raphael and all the other artists when he showed he was able

to overcome all the major difficulties in art. And it is true that these difficulties are mainly to be found in painting nudes and the foreshortening of the figures. But I believe that he could reply that, just as the subject, when behaving naturally, does not always assume a pose in which the artist, in order to depict him, has to make use of foreshortening, so there is no need for him to diligently seek foreshortened views in his painting whenever possible, and the same applies to the nudes, with rare exceptions. Thus, when the difficult things (and also things that are strange to see, as these are) are painted more rarely, they cause greater wonder and greater pleasure, too. So, in my opinion, foreshortening is more remarkable when the artist, because of the limited space available or the many copies of the figures that the composition requires, is able to fit many things into a small space; or simply when, because of the gestures, it is more convenient for him to foreshorten the arm, leg, hand, foot, head or any other part of the body, doing this carefully and with discretion, or, at times, simply to demonstrate his ability.
(Ludovico Dolce, *Lettera a Messer Gaspare Bellini*, Turin 1978)

I t was necessary to refer to at least two of the most important results in this field in order to understand the revolutionary innovations of the *Doni Tondo*, which is not set in a tondo, but rather in a globe. This is the sum total of the first innovation, but it is not merely a switch from plane geometry to stereometry: the transition is radical. Mastery

of the third dimension is precisely what a sculptor accustomed to working on a statue from all sides might possess. Mention must also be made of the colour. The picture, painted with pure tempera, is very well preserved: generally speaking, the colours are cold. The yellow of Joseph's mantle is toned down, and the red of Mary's tunic is dull; this marked the beginning of the reduction of colour to chiaroscuro, as is found in all Mannerist painting. Only the blue of Mary's mantle is bright, but its tone is icy. The nudes are roseate, but in the way that, in red chalk drawings, the red is not a colour. It is evident, therefore, that Michelangelo was seeking to neutralize the colour in order to focus the power of the spatial expression, with sharply defined plasticity that is strongly reminiscent of sculpture. It is sufficient to compare the folds in the drapery with those of the Piet in St. Peter's to see the close relationship: there is the same plastic intensity and the same independence from colour. In the Piet the white of the marble has the same value as the blues, reds and yellows of the *Doni Tondo*. In other words, these colours do not themselves have any value, but are subordinate to the form on which they appear.
The whole of the complex structure of the *Doni Tondo*—which is clearly Neoplatonic—may well have been conceived by Michelangelo himself, who was often inspired by Neoplatonism, not only in his sculptures, but also in his poetry; on the other hand, in Florence, this philosophical system was as all-pervading as air. And it is the superb way in which he has transformed the

abstract idea into sharply defined plastic forms which indicates that the preliminary programme was drawn up by the artist himself.
But even if it had been suggested to him, just as Poliziano had given many ideas to Botticelli, it would not reduce by one jot the astounding originality of this unique painting, which is one of the greatest human achievements, a treasure without equal that can only be evaluated in terms of the spirit—the human conscience that surpasses itself and, as Dante would have put it, "draws closer to God."
(Cesare Brandi, *Disegno della pittura italiana*, Turin 1980)

It is no coincidence that Ludovico Dolce's attack—just like Pietro Aretino's had been and Giovanni Gilio's would be—centred around the frescoes in the Sistine Chapel. It should be noted that these attacks were not wholly innocuous or platonic, if one bears in mind that, in the same period, Michelangelo's masterpiece ran the risk of being plastered over and was probably only saved thanks to the immense prestige that the artist still enjoyed; in any case, draperies were periodically painted over the nudes.
Just why was there so much intolerance of the genitals displayed so immodestly in the sanctum sanctorum of Catholicism? Analysed as a whole, and not only with regard to the passages specifically devoted to the *Last Judgement*, Dolce's *Aretino o Dialogo della pittura* can suggest what lay behind the scandalized reactions, or, rather, what they implied and foreboded. In fact, the calls for

"decorum" and "propriety" involved problems of much greater significance than these concepts seem to express at first sight. In addition to the scandal of the nudes, it is possible to discern the one regarding iconographic unorthodoxy; apart from the moral judgement, there was a political and aesthetic one. What was involved, consciously or otherwise, was, in other words, the general orientation that was being given to the "politics of the image," beginning with the redefinition of the sacred image and the establishment of new limits to the freedom of the artist in this field. These were the first signs of a procedure for controlling the image that became increasingly widespread and that, from the outset, revealed its tendency to digress from the question of contents to that of style—that is, from the purely iconographic realm to the aesthetic one.
From the first scandalized reactions, when Michelangelo was still working on the scaffolding in the Sistine Chapel, and Aretino's letter, right up to the Dolce's essay and Gilio's treatise, there was a constant process of cultural revision which was set in motion with the classic watchword—"decorum."
Situated in the centre of a historical vortex, Michelangelo frescoes were destined to constitute the sublime watershed, acclaimed, but also controversial, catalysing cultural and political tensions that were felt far beyond the purely artistic sphere.
It was no coincidence that a work like the *Last Judgement*—which is so sensitive due to both the theme treated and the place for which it was in-

tended—was commissioned at the time when the Curia was most receptive to the ideas of the "evangelical" currents of the Catholic Reformation, in the years at the end of Clement VII's pontificate and the beginning of that of Paul III.

This was a period in which it was hoped that a genuine reform, carried out from within, without cataclysms, but also without hesitation, could heal the dramatic rupture created in the church by the Reformation. It was the period of the Consilium de emendanda ecclesia (1536, the year in which Michelangelo began the *Last Judgement*) and the attempts to seek a dialogue with the Protestants, the protagonists of which were Cardinal Contarini, Reginald Pole and Iacopo Sadoleto. Similarly, it was not by chance that a work like the *Last Judgement*—the intense religious feeling of which is, however, both subjective and aristocratic— did not meet with the approval of the Counter-Reformation current that suddenly, about 1542, took the initiative, upsetting the delicate balance of power in the Curia and putting paid to hopes of reconciliation and the aspirations of the evangelical current in the higher echelons of the Church.

It was in this climate that, just as it was being praised to the skies, the *Last Judgement* was subjected to the first attacks concentrated in two directions: the polemic regarding the nude and the one regarding iconographic orthodoxy. The latter was a theme that, at times, emerged explicitly, while, at other times, it was concealed in the meanders of the prolix confutations of Michelangelo's creations, inter-

spersed with reminders of the need to avoid "obscurity," "poetic licence" and "historical incongruities" in the delicate domain of the sacred image.
(Antonio Pinelli, "La Maniera: definizione di campo e modelli di lettura," in *Storia dell'Arte,* VI, Turin 1980)

Undoubtedly Leonardo extended the field of knowledge—and the capacity of human beings to know— beyond all limits. He conceived nature as becoming, thus as a movement, or, rather, a furor that was, at the same time, cosmological, physiological and psychological. And he proposed knowledge of the world, both as the object and the subject, through penetrating analyses rather than by mirroring representation. But, by extending the limits to infinity, he strengthened the naturalistic concept of art: in the ideology of the Renaissance, his phenomenal and analytical naturalism was the secular parallel and the analytical and experimental complement to the dogmatic and historicist naturalism of Raphael.

Although it was apparently conservative, the contrary standpoint of Michelangelo was, in reality, daringly advanced. His synthesis of the arts was neither the fusion of similar entities nor a compendium of the universe, but the outcome of a dialectical process. He was aware that synthesis was not only unity of the arts, but also isolation of art in the system of culture, which was no longer unified. He saw that poetry, and probably music, were integrated into the independent, but intercommunicating, domain of art, but nothing else associ-

ated it with other disciplines, science to begin with. The removal of the basic principle of mimesis meant denying the value of representation as a cognitive act. Certainly, Leonardo had already denied it, but in order to indicate other, more incisive ways of acquiring knowledge. Michelangelo did not accept the dogma of art as mimesis simply because he considered art to be the effect of a cause, thus giving it a logical, dual structure that his ontological monism rejected. Besides, if nature was created by God in his own image, then there was all the more reason why it should not be represented, because the relationship of mortals with God should be one of love and aspiration, that is, inductive and not deductive.

In Michelangelo's case, his commitment to his work and the events in his life cannot be separated. It should not be cause for surprise that, because failure would have meant ruin, from the moment he was given the responsibility for the completion of St. Peter's, he did not think of anything else. And yet figurative art was abandoned consciously, or even deliberately, as he states in his poems and letters. The appointment coincided with— and is explained by—the most acute moment of what was described as his conversion, when the chronic intellectual tension was becoming a religious vocation. It seemed to him then that "sculpting so many statues" was due to mental laziness, an assumption that God was similar to human beings: what else were nature and the figure if not a third term, a form of mediation, an allegorical fiction interposed between the subject and object of a relationship of love? The soul that had been converted and offered to God with the approach of death no longer expressed itself with metaphors. But the transition from the mimetic images of figurative art to the metapsychic ones of architecture did not mean vanishing into abstraction. Increasingly more laden with messages, the image became more intense and scrupulously irrelative, like a jewel in a precious setting. God, too, may be seen with the eyes: if only Michelangelo could have been all eyes in order to see him better.

In order to see him, the dead will regain their eyes before the *Last Judgement*. And the visibility of the Church had a theological motive.

(Giulio Carlo Argan, *Michelangelo architetto*, Milan 1990)

Essential Bibliography

J. S. Ackerman, *The Architecture of Michelangelo*, 2 vols., Viking, London 1961; 2nd ed., 1 vol. (paperback), Penguin Books, Harmondsworth 1971.

G. C. Argan, B. Contardi, *Michelangelo architetto*, Milan 1990.

U. Baldini, *The Complete Sculpture of Michelangelo*, Thames and Hudson, London 1982.

L. Bellosi, *Michelangelo pittore*, Florence 1970.

A. Condivi, *Life of Michelangelo*, ed. Helmut Wohl, Phaidon, Oxford 1976.

B. Contardi, G.C. Argan, "Michelangelo," in *Art Dossier*, no. 9, Florence 1985.

H. von Einem, *Michelangelo*, London 1973; paperback edition, London 1976, New York 1977.

Ettlinger, L.D., *The Complete Paintings of Michelangelo*, Classics of World Art, London and New York 1969.

L. Goldscheider, *Michelangelo: Paintings, Sculptures, and Architecture*, 5th ed., Phaidon, London 1975.

F. Hartt, *The Paintings of Michelangelo*, Thames and Hudson, London 1965.

F. Hartt, *Michelangelo, the Complete Sculptor*, Thames and Hudson, London 1969.

F. Hartt, *The Drawings of Michelangelo*, New York 1970 and London 1971.

H. Hibbard, *Michelangelo*, New York and London 1975.

L. Murray, *Michelangelo*, Thames and Hudson, London 1980.

L. Murray, *Michelangelo, His Life, Work and Times*, Thames and Hudson, London 1984.

L. Steinberg, *Michelangelo's Last Paintings*, London and New York 1975.

G. Vasari, Giorgio, *The Lives of the Artists*, translated by J. Conaway Bondanella and P. Bondanella, Oxford University Press, Oxford and New York 1991.